NOVENA

Jacques J. Rancourt

NOVENA

PLEIADES
P R E S S

Lena-Miles Wever Todd Poetry Series

Warrensburg, Missouri

Library of Congress Control Number:
ISBN: 978-0-8071-6660-4

Published by Pleiades Press

Department of English
University of Central Missouri
Warrensburg, Missouri 64093

Distributed by Louisiana State University Press

Cover Image: Anita Cruz-Eberhard, "Digital Ikebana #15." Digital
photography, archival pigment print. 13 x 19 in. Edition 5(&2AP), 2008.
Used with permision from West Collection, Oaks, PA and Cooper +
Dyer Art Collection, Alexandria, VA.

Book design by Sarah Nguyen
Author's photo by Danny Chung
First Pleiades Printing, 2017

Financial support for this project has been provided by a UCM Foun-
dation Opportunity Grant and the Missouri Arts Council, a state
agency.

for my parents

and in memoriam M.C.W.

Table of Contents

HELLO MY NAME IS ALSO JACQUES RANCOURT

So you already know we've placed ourselves in the nape
of the rake. Copper harp. Sickle-
                         tongued. You know
each year we've braided strands of wheat into rope

to tie about our necks. My father, a Jacques Rancourt too,
split back the wormed casing
                         of a rotted tree to remind me
we open into fields. Dry haven. Corned breath. My father

doesn't speak the language he grew up speaking.
We who are nearly the same
                         clear one space out of
the next. My father's father, a Jacques Rancourt too,

broke open an American forest into fallow. Felling saw.
Bucking saw. Two-man saw. I am the Jacques
                         of a Jacques
of a Jacques who sent home dead goldfinches in the mail.

Lumber and tar sap. Tilt into the axis of our galaxies.
My father Jacques and myself Jacques
                         cannot pronounce
our own names properly. In the photograph we look

nearly the same. Heft and hewn. In the photograph
a Jacques Rancourt, the father
                         of my father, stands on the hulk
of a felled white pine, his two-man saw cast off,

and who among us takes up the other end?

BLACK HORSE

A squirrel tumbling from evergreens,
a chord of upset in the hemlocks—my mother also knew me
         as a vine shivering up a stick,
a goose bobbing through wintry mist. He's touched,

      she said, so I surrendered to the field
outside my house, stomping crop circles in the neck-high grass,
            my thoughts hummingbirds tonguing syrup. My father,
      the black horse, studied me, a white horse

      painted black, now shivering in the rain,
now mouth-colored paint stammering down my hooves.
            Time to grow up, he said,

      but I wouldn't—I was an insect trapped in amber,
a goose feather under ice, a hummingbird in the throat,
            a whinny through the pines.

IN THE BEGINNING

Manliness was a continent with trees
    and I did push-ups under its boughs
until I couldn't. During those years

    I masturbated endlessly, amazed
by what my body could create. Early canvas—
    fingers brushing stone, nine deer

charging four hunters. I'd never seen
    the bucks that wander outside
my house—only their tracks

    and droppings at the edge of the lawn.
I had to find them, which left me
    chasing snapped branches through

the woods, searching for a stag
    that straddled a ledge, a father
who always watched, a slice of land

    that crowned the horizon.
This my night fire, my ashy dawn—
    a dove transformed into a mourning dove

and flicked into the air, going from boat
    to nowhere to boat, until one day
it stops, drops an olive branch at my feet.

SONG FOR THE HOMEBOUND MEN

A helix of gull squall, all drove and dip,

     plucks Odysseus like a harp.
Through the flutter and oar spirals,

     the sirens sing naked

on the shore. In this variation
     the sirens are male,

their bodies exposed like oysters,

     their sheen revealing the flesh
of what Odysseus never knew

     he wanted. They reach for him

who reaches with wrists still tied to the mast,
     his chest a swarm of pollock.

Now seals prod the sea. Now his crew

     wheel paddles overhead,
brine splattering their shirtlessness.

     Now Odysseus's feet curl

into questions. Unbind me, he says
     and they bind him faster.

Clutched mast, dry-wood splinters,

     his blood flowing freely now,
he looses the song inside his chest,

     a music box the wind tips open—

THE OFFERING

That night the shore kept our sneakers,
the branches our boxers. Slapping
each other's backs, tossing a ball
between us, it was a test of manhood,
to see how naked we'd get
and not care. Jon, the most beautiful,
was laughing, and through the water
I saw his pale blur. When the girls
came with their reluctance to leave
their panties in the tree shrine, the water rose.
We brushed against each other,
sent beer cans crumpled downriver

until, from the other side, branches broke,
a tree line shiver rustled the darkness.
A deer had come to taste the shore
and was frozen at the edge, as I was,
until we bolted away. Into the field
I ran with the pack and saw Jon, all of him,
holding the hand of a girl. They bounded
toward the foggy proof of town,
but I had left my reflection at the shore,
the deer's too, my other's arm
outstretched and offering water.

THE GATE

Redeemed for a moment
like the martyr with his cocked head,

his shoulder dislocating,
it was not the first time I heard angels

filling the humid places,
the Angel of Relief holding my face

in the garden to comfort me who-was-called,
a child on the cusp of all

that thereafter. Along marshlands,
my feet flickering along the wet path,

in the salt reek, the putrid fish
half-gorged, the wading birds behind a bush

rising up in front of the monastery,
that house of light, my house of tainted stained light

and stolen relics—shard of saint bone,
I am told—

I found behind ivy the weeping statue,
and found myself again going to

confession for the fourth
time that month, into its dark mouth

at the end of childhood,
closing the gate of childhood:

When did you last touch yourself?—

the priest's coarsely-shaved chin leaning
against the filigree of that screen—

and how?

BACKYARD ROCK

That year, I learned to float by filling my body
with questions. Night swimming with my father
was the first time
                    since the fog of childhood I'd seen
a man naked. The lake thickened with bloodsuckers,
the moon a sliver in the sky—
                              uncut, tucked within
a hood of skin, unlike mine, his tip like the backyard rock
split in three. Think of Ham
                              who too saw the nakedness
of his father. Think of God enlarging Japheth. It was both
what I did
            and did not want. How I understood myself
uneasily as my own dim reflection, uselessly as my shadow
cast at night.

                              *

It happened, I'm told, because water trickled down
a crack and froze,
                    expanded and split apart this rock
or boulder, whenever a rock becomes a boulder,
in millimeters, then inches,
                              then feet. I walk this path
through the rock, and where one side indents,
the other extends, so that one could push it back
together again
                if one were God. On the northern cut,
my fire glows and the ice on the trees around me rears up
like a question, like a knife.

                              *

I have summoned the hair I know exists inside to sprout
across my chest like his, I've culled the same slate rocks

and still my body, newly unbuilt and barren.
My father and I share our name
                              yet he goes by *Jack.*
I want to believe we're still tied to the same chicken wire
but here I am—here we are—
                              the earth undigging its graves,
the clouds wringing out their water. The day I convinced
a squirrel to eat from my hand, its tiny nail-feet sticky
with sap, I could have
                              if I was that kind of person
snapped its leg simply by closing my fist. Could have
even if I was not.

*

Walking at night in winter, I'm headed away
from an encounter with a man I've met on the internet.
When he asks for a name,
                              I give him *Jack.* My father,
drunk and lolling in a hammock, once told me
his first time was with an older woman
and three other boys. I mull this over by way of ice.
Bed, breed, burrow:
                              two mammals leap in
and out an old fishing hole. I step closer;
the frozen lake protests.
                              Too small to be beavers,
too large to be muskrats, they leap in and out.
I step closer; the frozen lake, a dark marble,
clouded and cracked,
                              protests. It's not a fishing hole,
I realize, but the edge of ice—beyond them
black open water—and for once in my life I can measure
how closely I stand
                              to the periphery of danger.

*

I believe in the father and the ease he raised

fire with, using only
                    the leaves around him, an act
I couldn't do with gasoline. I believe in the glory
of the day birds at midnight,
                              the egret that follows
the swallow, the sand crabs that corkscrew up
the salt marshes. I believe I first learned lust
by watching
              the men in my family swim,
and even now that boyhood water still feels like silk.
I believe the day will come
                      when this too feels ordinary.

                    *

Out on the frozen lake stripped blank as a face,
out where the ice heaves
                    beneath me, a groan
or a snap, and at five inches deep I know it will hold
I know it will
              even if my knees—the sweat pilling
my fleece—does not,
                    out in the sun-lock, the ice-blister
of the day, out where I watch the trap I've set
sit and stay,
              drawn low below me while trout
tangle under the ice in a diamond of a dance,
out where my father had stood, his boot-prints glazed
by snow and rain,
                  out where his traps snapped up
at once, a fish's frenzy to yank down the cords,
to impale their flap-cheeks on the barbs
and feel that sting,
                    that pull into air, their blood
patterning the snow in scales, I understand
I am not my father,
                  not earlier today by the woodshed,
by his fell, sailing an axe over my shoulder
and into the block of wood

                         where it plants, shakes loose,
the log still standing solid, unsplit, and whole:
I try to understand how if
                         I hack and hack, the log
will come apart in pieces, strips, first bark and slivers,
but eventually, as it must, it will halve
                                  and halve again.

*

NOVENA

1.

Ave Maria beneath the boardwalk, I will never tell
what I saw past the sunbathers laid out like sewage,
between the salty pillars. You led me there

where you slid your silicone breasts up from
your tunic into your most holy hands.
Lady Maria, teach me to pray. I am a child

and do not know how. Move my lips until I believe
a man can kiss a man like this, until I know how
to praise the gulls' resounding hymn, the rollers' thrum.

2.

Thrummed by cypress branches, Sweet Lady
of the Juniper Berries: my mother placed me
in your January arms, gave me to your breathless chest

the day I walked out into the helix
of a snow sprawl, into the spindle of an eye undone.
You prostrated me beneath a barbwire fence,

my jacket snagged on its hooks.
The tabernacle of your arms, Holy Mother,
its gilded doors the open mouth of without.

3.

Goat blood over the open mouths of doors, the sky
split by a volcano, a candle lit to remind me
I too could melt like bricks, become a tephra fossil

in the garden. While fire chases the city,
I wait for ashes. This rapture hallelujah,
this inferno goddamn, and the angel of death

checking each window with a Maglite. With blinds drawn,
the light stripes us, and we make love like zebras.
Our punk-rock mohawks, our fingers lightly touching.

4.

Beata Vergine, touch the parts of me
most faithful. Accept my hymn, my feeble limning.
With dawn stretched across our foreheads

and the sound of a wave in the highest room
drowning my pharaohs—Lady, I will dance with you
in the streets until a show of hummingbirds swarms

beneath your hem and chants Gregorian to the morning.
You are our life, our nectar, our agave's bluest spear.
Hail Holy Queen, I will love you ruby-throated.

5.

Salve Regina, there's a pistol down my throat,
a magazine cocked in my hand. See
what I have done. I came to him in the night

while my parents were sleeping, past amaryllises,
past grapes frozen on a trellis. I came rosaries
onto his chest. He was a gun, a game

of Russian roulette. Laying on a moon
like scorpions under a star-studded sheet, my breath
dismantled, our barbs leaked venom.

6.

Owl squawk and sumac, the bough's barb
snaps back to the tree. Eve, the first Mary,
slowly chews the peach that bruises

in her hand. When she swallows the pit whole,
no surprise, it bulges her throat, an Adam's apple,
an egg-eating snake. Now a sprout clouts her cleft,

a shaft now fruits, her breasts deflate;
now Adam's all weepy. Wind hissing leaves,
the forest is alive with the Deerman's blinking.

7.

The Deerman in a suit beaded with burrs,
tie tight at his neck. He lives behind leaves,
behind bark, in the bat hollows of trees. Thighs and cock

he offers. Sancta Maria in the moonlight:
nearing a grove of nettles and moonflowers
I crush mushrooms with my knees

in my blue stumble toward your feet. Constantly
I kiss them. Between your toes, a garden snake writhes,
its antlered tongue a flag tantrum by wind.

8.

Hail Mary full of thunder, hail on my windshield,
the spider-twitch to my ear. These your most
winding roads, begotten—not made—of ice

and corn flowers. Hail Mary in the gorge stream,
in the glacier meadows, my prayers
are flowers between your toes, small ones,

mayflowers, lavender and fragile. Light blueing
the hues of my skin, we may have kissed
in the car but only to stay warm.

9.

I saw you once through a warm flush
of smoke at a bar. You were the drag queen dressed
as Tina Turner crooning soul into

a microphone. Your drunk rendition
of *Proud Mary*, your excessive lips quivering.
Cigarette incense, faux-hawk cathedrals,

we assumed you into the floodlights.
Fierce advocate of our hearts,
remember us when you come again.

*

ACT OF CONTRITION

Two people who are honest
for the first time speak

honestly to each other:
There are flocks of sheep

herding dogs inside me;
there are lovers I've pared

from apples with knives.
This season of smut

split up into two
until the body could have

what the body
was not allowed. In winter

I became one part driven
to fleas and mange, teeth,

the other part left foaming
over. The sky then pink

as the underside of my tongue.
Pink as the skin beneath

the dead fox's fur. Lover,
I've firmly resolved

to amend my life,
but I keep breaking.

OPEN SHED

When I took off into the woods behind my house
where the dusk lays down like a wolf, my mother prayed
I would be kept put. Snow had melted into bogs
twice as deep as I was tall and children in our town
were always drowning. Answered prayer: a volunteer,
our town's only barber, found me pinned down beneath
the claws of a barbwire fence. It took hours
to be found. No helicopter could see me through
the cover of oaks. No dog could sniff me out
because I did not smell like the living. When the news
told stories of teenagers who took their own lives,
took them as if they were something to be carried for a while
and then dropped, I could understand. In the woods
behind my house, the animals were always dying:
the foxes I found crisscrossed against the stone wall;
the moose's rack that reared up from the mulch, bugs picking
skin off its skull. And like the wind that kicks up
the brush, that turns over all the trees' leaves at once,
what began as frightening soon dulls into nothing.

Between my house and the woods, there was a shed.
I had dreams of sleeping in there while outside
the wolves paced. I went inside once, the ice stiffening
the hinges, and I found tools, a bench. But up above,
a white owl, large as a boy and frozen
to the rafters, stared down at me. And I stared back.
Now, whenever I hear the wolves cry, it reminds me
I am still afraid to die. A strange comfort,
that chill. When the barber brought me out of the fog
and into my mother's arms, it was not her boy he returned.
Snared on the fence, facedown to the ground and watching
the Witch-hazel in front of me, its unstoppable flowers,
my mother echoing off the trunks of trees, I kept
to the dirt, not ready—not yet—to get up and return.

THE ORDAINED

Once snow has filled the lungs, it takes some time
to cover the body. Though winter hounds

the animals, it waits to scrub them down
the trees, and my vocation was to wait,

my marriage vow a veil, in this my state
of tight-packed snow. If God were a season

then he would surely be winter, would ground
by starvation, frostbite, and he would bait

in pairs. I outwitted God by haunting
bear-empty caves and feeding off their pawn,

stripping a tree into a rib-thin wife.
I gave my soul to God but he wanted

my body. I gave to winter what belonged
to winter. The rest I cut free with a knife.

HISTORY

In that endless season of dead grass and rot,
I stood in a tree and named the cows
in the field beside my house
after brands of sodas. I'd go to Jeb's

when his mother was out
and we'd wear her silk nightgowns.
Basketball boobs, stitches stretched,
we lip-synced as Celine and Whitney,

dancing breast to breast, a distance
we couldn't close. Our hands
at the chorus—*You were history*
with the slamming of the door—reached

for our chests, each other's chests,
the floor. The gowns we discarded
on the table, the sky purpling
past dusk. When he asked me to stay

because his mother wasn't home yet
he understood the looming weight
of the world, unlike me who flapped
through my childhood carelessly

as a flag. How could I know
his father raped him? I left him there,
biking home in the rising dark,
and because I had no language

for the wind I couldn't see, I spent hours
in that tree naming all the cows
7-Up, Mountain Dew, Royal Crown,
Moxie, Sprite, Orange Crush.

BOUNDING WET DARK

and the fields are wet too,
the grass, the questions

we press together to answer.

You are the last candle from the barn
I blow out. Sunday wish,

we are alive

only a short time. What is the purpose
of a field if not to lie in it?—

So we make the field

a field, myself
nothing more. Grasshoppers leaping

out of sight, I already know

what won't happen. The night
pales at the pine scrim. We lie

beneath rotting stars.

THE DISTANCE

Blankets on the roof, the early sun
surrounding the hills—I want
to be happy. When I think of your hair
in my mouth, the wedge that gives us,

that morning in April and the flock
of birds below—blackbirds, maybe,
or just birds that are black—I think
of how the light shut our eyelids

tight as moth buds. As always
I lose focus. There were hills we stared at
sun-blinded. There was a plane
lifting in the sky, a vanishing,

long wings and the last stream
of exhaust. In the distance
a bell rang and children filed inside.
In the distance my arm resolved

around your waist. Were you on my right
or my left? There were children
in the schoolyard, coyotes dotting the hills,
sparrows on the belfry, or crows.

SPLAKE

My father casts a line, three colors deep,
and trolls. It's cold. I zip my coat
up to my chin, think how I could be asleep
but here we are, a part of the fact.
We are waiting for something to catch.
We are trying. He's grown older, my father,
his face an echo. The insects hatch:
they live to mate, mate to die. Down further
from us, a tree has given over
and slumps in the water, the river floor
a city of decomposed trees. The motor
chokes, the line tugs, I pull and pull more.
An afterlife? The splake jerks its head,
slaps the boat's bench even after it's dead.

AMERICAN SHRAPNEL

I'm aware of the dead's hands on my shoulders,
their shoulders
                    torn by barbs and bottles, hands that lead
but do not aid. In the blue before morning

I come across you, and because I want someone
to kiss me
                I lock eyes with you like a sickle
locks wheat, like it pulls. The dead are not surprised

when you toss me from the chain links
to the brickyard. I've known
                                this day would come
when my faith would be tested:

Are you a Christian? A man? A fag?
No, the cock crows,
                    my grandfather unfolds
his fingers, gives me a gift from the war:

a cartridge case, and inside the case, a statue
of Mary. You fit my neck
                            into your elbow,
give my jaw to the curb—before I was born

I wasn't. Before morning the air smells like aspirin.
Be careful. My skull is full
                            of petition, a shell
inside a shell: a cartridge case, a battered virgin

in the shape of a bullet.

*

NOVENA

1.

Here you are again, Our Lady of Crocuses,
sleeping on hay, frocked in camelhair with no inn
to shave your face. You take off your wig

and hold your baby while your common-law husband
bends toward the horizon, uneasy. Magi wind, too-bright star:
he tosses the wig at you who are most beautiful

with nails painted and eyebrows plucked.
Guarding against glances, he keeps these things quiet
as straw, swallowing half the truth whole.

2.

The flesh of crabs swallowed whole by seagulls
black with oil, the beach pocked by their hollowed husks—
Ave Maria in the hurricane, you stomp

the seaboard's billow in hallowed heels,
your cloak ballooning with pity. Wave-beaten rocks,
this steadfast of *good enough* I hold onto. The surf

smacks against your phantom form. You're always
almost here, your feet wreathing with mollusks
and shells, your eyes two whirlpools draining.

3.

Our Lady of Tornadoes, you whirl through plains
spreading bales across the Midwest, your hair
a flock rushing after seeds. At noon I chant

the Angelus: *pray for us, pray for us, pray for us.*
I wait. A prairie mantled with shingles,
a dancer's hair caught in branches.

In snow, Gabriel mouths: Blessed are you
among women and blessed is the orange
you hold, its rind a fire in your palm.

4.

Hail Mary caught on fire. The drapes, the tablecloth,
the knots in the rug on fire. I'm desperately
on fire. Kitchen floor collecting trails of ash

from my burning shirt, fire hearths
the heart of pine boards. The Deerman watching
as I crawl backwards, the rug bunching

in folds. His boots clopping wood, his eyes on me
like eyes. Holy Mary, of course you lurk
in the corners. Of course, you do nothing.

5.

Pummel and surge coarse my throat, the sea stormed
by a fleet of deer, tossing me against their sides,
pasterns against my back, my nostrils

punctured by water. Lightning on the ceiling
furious with their kicking, I sink to the ocean's
bottom where you, covered in algae, reach

with both hands. Ave Maria, your feet are sunk
in seaweed, your eyes clot with salt, yet you
hardly blink. Above us, stags cross waves and waves.

6.

Mater Dei, your immaculate heart waived
like mine, your plum-sack organ pierced by a sword.
He raked his teeth across my throat in the attic.

Via Dolorosa—the long drag down the stairs,
against the steps, pulling me backward
into the basement, pinning me back down.

Futile prayer: I've returned to vegetables
beneath the reach of roots. Your watching did less
than the wind outside which blew the Salix.

7.

Blue cloak, blue desire over the horizon,
you are our handmaiden pulling milk from a well,
magnifying the Lord and the Godsperm glowing

fiercely in your womb. Magnificat in the blue morning:
by now, you're dogsledding through fields
and the yawning dawn, lines of fence posts,

pads of wolf feet slapping. The ghost of me praying
returns, unwanting this: the anvil of
what had been taken, of what had not been offered.

8.

My heart offered on a plate. The Deerman watches
two shadows: dog and dog eating. They pull its sinew
and when it snaps, it snaps their snouts.

Smoke and tar flesh, I watch its stretching,
my transubstantiation into dog food. Madonna
performing on stage with a boa constricting necklace—

yours is the applause, the cameras coruscating,
the crowds arresting their wrists while backstage
it has begun: the wet slurping of my dread.

9.

Our Lady with Dreadlocks, I watch from behind
curtains as you sit before your mirror,
a twelve-bulb crown, and slide the wig off your scalp.

Your upturned cups resting on the cosmetic table,
stubble returning to you like spring grass.
When you discover me in the reflection,

you tell me to come closer. Mother, into your lap
I submit my face, and we hold each other like men.
Stroke my hair now and at the hour of my death.

*

FIELD

In the field where I'm always returning,
in the jaundice, in the wheat, I am eight
and we stomp stems with our running.
Hand that bears no mercy, I ask for none.
In the field where I spend the afternoon
in the Y-crook of a tree, I've been crying.
Mama Bird, hold me quietly. Our lawn's
littered by the car, Papa's oiled hands
that repair, the cigarette that spills
on the motor. I'm expected to help
but under my skirt I hold secrets.
Hand that does not seek to understand,
here is my face; here is the rest of me.
My sister and I pretend in the wheat
where we hide our childhood, lying
in its itch long after we should.
World of wonder, world of fireflies
and satellites: our world is small
and always shrinking. I take the skirt
from my sister, slip it on to feel
its swish of silk around my thighs, and run
through the field where I'm always
returning, its flag dragging behind me.
My sister and I are just pretending:
you be the Mama Bird and I'll be the chick;
you be the hand that knows and I'll be
broken on the linoleum floor.
Hand that gives swift reply, answer me now.
We sit in the sandbox the cat thinks
is litter, and my sister makes me eat each one;
it is the nature of our play, my obedience.
In the distance a windmill sounds
like declaration: *We are, we are, we are.*
While we pretend in a field that's more
of a stage, Diesel Papa has had enough

and the skirt is taken, my mouth left sour.
Hand of insurrection that resurrects the hem,
return my self to myself. I retake it
from the closet, hide in the field that betrays
while Papa's body is occupied inside
the cavity of a Chevy. The bluster dries,
makes sails of my skirt, and in the distance
the windmill sounds like heartbeats.

SEDGE

In revisiting the Book of Mistakes,
there's first the violation, the volition of the tree—
branches shorn, a corridor cut to the sky,
the memory of you made real by the sun.
We are what's left of that dream of a place.
Herald flowers, a vine growing out of a lock
like a tongue, I tell you I've been there,
the overgrown fields of my paradise, and back,

and am more alone for having gone.
Grass so sharp it cuts our shins, I loved you most
when there was some semblance of the real—
pain, beads of blood—that made me look
outside the dream, at the globe of the sky
already deteriorating. The facts
I don't remember. Only how it felt to remember
the moments I was pulled out.

THE DROUGHT

Oakland, California

Admittedly I was wrong
about ambivalence, the buildings
coming out of fog
above the garden, the geese
inconsolably clinging to winter.
You were away from home
minding the dead. My physician,
your life will never be quite
your own. Meanwhile, I jogged the rim
of the lake. Backdrop: day filled
as if with gun smoke, night
with helicopters, the spears
of their sight tracking the highways,
the streets. It's easy now
to imagine a police state, a country
ruled by guns, and who has them,
and who has more of them.
On your balcony, you played
Beethoven to drown out
their droning. Nocturne, eerie night:
We knew by morning
more would be shot. December,
the sun dimmed quicker,
the helicopters returned—
you at the hospital,
in your bed, on your balcony,
at the bench of your piano,
and I wanted more
than ever to be touched.

MONOGAMY

Last of all I find the garden with its thousand steps.
    How many times have I walked by
and never seen the two staircases widening out away
    before coming back together, over and over?
I walk through the garden—tiger lilies, painted roses,
    though the season for flowers has past—
there are worse bonds to break than the body's—
    the stairs are empty, the night comes quickly,
the steps, the sentinel stone crows wet
    from an afternoon rain—*some animals*
understand this—and when I reach the top—
    others will brood a stone if it stays beneath them—
I walk out to a part of the city
    where I have never walked.

WHAT GOD HAS DIVIDED LET NO MAN UNITE

I know this corner like it's mine,
this corner that belongs to all
who have ever called it their own.
I know this sidewalk, cracks
and all. I know thresher stare
and I know flip wrist. I ride

this train to the end of the line
because back home a pipe burst
and now water trickles down
my wall, now my ceiling darkens
and cracks, writes fate
over my bed. At night I'm taken

out of sleep by the break
of a drop on my nose.
On the train a stranger and I
exchange a look. Not lust,
not exactly, but an understanding—
you who are alone

are never alone. The city sets
in Apple and Hanes and never
have I felt this tired
or this complete. The earth turns
and I begin my long decay.
The earth turns each day.

THE SAME WORD

Last night I watched the drag queen's hip-pad
drift down her leg
                            and distort the full moon
of her figure. By dawn you won't recall
how I hummed her song to you while you were sleeping.
We call this a marriage, but it isn't
                                    called that outside
this room. It isn't called a thing. I've searched for a word
that means what I mean it to—how we are a part
of the world as much as we are apart from it—

and it does not exist. Still, we make of this thing
an imitation, an effigy. Still, we make it each day
because we exist, weary phantom, as both the flesh
and the illusion,
                            because we live together
even if we live as a drag queen does, drawing
applause from a world that holds her at bay.

PROOF OF LIGHT

It's the come-after, the spine
of a feather. It exists, I know,
because I can see you
tick open in degrees,
and I'm afraid to wake you
and take what you need.
It's the marshes in winter,
the reeds sheathed in ice.
It's where we stare each other
down for hours, the rain
that glazes our eyelids and mouths.
It's who I pray to when I need
the dark. It's the starling
that falls from the murmur.
It's the summer I jogged
through the forest, and a fawn—
just born and still wet—
stumbled through and licked my hand.
Don't you see? It came to me.
It licked my hand. And I
wanted it to. The mother
somewhere on her side, still open
and asleep, it's what I had to do—
I scared the fawn, I laid down
the hierarchy of fear
because that's what it needed
even if it's not what I want.
Because it'd been born now
and could see.

NO MIRACLE, NO ACT OF GOD

What should not stay unsaid will grow wild
as chicory flowers, as the mushrooms
on the damp side of a tree. In that time after sunrise
but before the light hits the shore, that time animals know,
my father took me in his canoe onto Greenwood Pond.
Passing by Flint's cabin and the A-frames,

we saw a doe's body lying in the shallows
where the reeds have grown high. A gunshot wound
in her left side browned the water, which was strange,
my father said, because it wasn't hunting season.
Strange because it was five in the morning
and the wound still bled. That night I dreamt

about a forest fire and all the animals of the earth
either running toward it or from it
because there were no other ways to go.
Once, I rode my bike down a hill into
the side of a shed because I felt for the first time
that invincible charge coursing through me

or because I didn't, because I never have,
not even at ten, and when the shed grew closer,
I held out my hand to protect myself, or to say *No*,
to say *This will not happen*, what no miracle, no act of God
could stop. It was physics: motion and speed
and impact. My palm hit the shed

then my palm hit my forehead, my elbow still locked,
the bone snapped back. In the moments before
my voice formed a cry, I lay on the ground and laughed
because I was alive. No one should be this glad
to be broken. The doe in the lake, water filling her nostrils,
was she glad? Or the hunter who watched the shapes

the moon made through the trees—was he glad
when the doe bounded up twice, then fell,
flopped in the water, the splash not as loud as the gun
but as deafening? Was he glad before that,
in the woods past dark, when she stepped into light?
In that same town, a woman was killed Thanksgiving morning

while hanging laundry out to dry. It was early,
the cold frosting the grass, and because it was cold
she wore white gloves, which looked to a different hunter
through the forest of dead birches to be the white
of a deer's tail. Two hunters in the same town,
and if they were glad, then why, both times,

did they leave the doe? It's easy to believe in God
when you live below mountains, covered by the shadow
of something larger. My father and I hiked up a mountain,
and on the way up we didn't speak, and on its crown
we said even less. No revelation: only the clouds,
and the trees, and the clouds overlapping the trees,

but there was something I wanted to tell him,
not knowing what it was. Lately I've been having
the same dream, the one where the moon
lights up all the white in the world and the doe
with the gunshot wound in her side runs toward the lake
to swim to that island off shore. But she does not make it,

takes two giant leaps in the shallows and reeds, and falls,
and for hours she watches the moon slip through the sky
and behind the mountain. And when the moon is hidden,
all goes dark. And the spots on the doe's back blow out
like candles. And the hunter is gone, scared by what
he's done. And the doe is alone except for the otter

that slips in at the shore, except for the loon that wails
its grief. In this dream, I know the doe is my father,
which doesn't make sense, but I know it's true,
so I bend down in the water beside the doe and stroke

her head. Dear dying doe, dear wet father—stay
a little longer. There is something I needed to tell you.

NOTES

"Hello My Name Is Also Jacques Rancourt": The line "Tilt into the axis of our galaxies" is translated and adapted from the Parisian poet Jacques Rancourt's "Fil d'Horizon."

"Novena": A *novena* is a Catholic prayer said over nine consecutive days that seeks intercession from the Virgin Mary, who is believed to serve as a conduit between the human and spiritual world. This sequence borrows some of its language from Marian Catholic rites, such as the Rosary and the Angelus, and owes its form to Jeffrey Thomson's poem "Blind Desire."

"History" is after Lynda Hull.

"The Distance": The last line is adapted from Derek Walcott.

ACKNOWLEDGMENTS

I would like to thank the Wallace Stegner program at Stanford University, the Wisconsin Institute for Creative Writing at the University of Wisconsin-Madison, the University of Maine-Farmington's creative writing program, the Bread Loaf Writers' Conference, and the Cité Internationale des Arts in Paris for their gifts of time, mentorship, and support.

To my teachers Quan Barry, Eavan Boland, Simone DiPiero, Ken Fields, Amaud Jamal Johnson, Jesse Lee Kercheval, Patricia O'Donnell, D.A. Powell, Lee Sharkey, Jeffrey Thomson, and Ronald Wallace: my appreciation and admiration.

To Kathryn Nuernberger and everyone at Pleiades Press, thank you for your careful attention in bringing this book to life. To Hadara Bar-Nadav, thank you for your faith in this collection.

My love and gratitude to my friends for their eyes and ears on this book, especially Brandon Crooks, Kai Carlson-Wee, Louisa Diodato, Rebecca Hazelton, Richie Hofmann, Josh Kalscheur, Christopher Kempf, Chaney Kwak, Nancy Reddy, Casey Thayer, Corey Van Landingham, and Greg Wrenn. A very special thank you to Brittany Cavallaro, who has read and reread all of my poems with discernment.

And finally to Walter Cheng, whose love buoys me, and to my parents— this book is for you.

Poems in this collection previously appeared in:

32 Poems: "Black Horse"
Adroit Journal: "The Ordained"
Beloit Poetry Journal: "Field"
Boxcar Review: "The Offering"
Drunken Boat: "Novena [Ave Maria beneath the boardwalk...]"
Gulf Coast: "Act of Contrition"
The Journal: "No Miracle, No Act of God"
Kenyon Review: "The Same Word"
Linebreak: "Song for the Homebound Men"

Memorious: "The Gate"
Michigan Quarterly Review: "Backyard Rock"
Narrative: "The Distance" and "Hello My Name Is Also Jacques Rancourt"
New England Review: "What God Has Divided Let No Man Unite"
The Paris-American: "Bounding Wet Dark"
Pleiades: "The Drought" and "Sedge"
Southeast Review; PN Review (UK): "American Shrapnel"
Southern Humanities Review: "Monogamy"
Two Weeks: A Digital Anthology of Contemporary Poetry: "In the Beginning"
Virginia Quarterly Review: "History"
West Branch: "Novena [Here you are again...]"
ZYZZYVA: "Open Shed" and "Proof of Light"

"Open Shed" was reprinted in *Best New Poets 2014.* "Backyard Rock"
was reprinted in *Be Wilder: A Word Portland Anthology.*

ABOUT THE AUTHOR

Jacques J. Rancourt was born in Maine. His poems have been recognized with a Stegner fellowship from Stanford, the Halls Emerging Artist Fellowship from the Wisconsin Institute for Creative Writing, and a residency from the Cité Internationale des Arts in Paris. His poems have appeared in the *Kenyon Review, New England Review, Ploughshares, Virginia Quarterly Review,* and *Best New Poets 2014.* He lives and teaches in the San Francisco Bay Area.

THE LENA-MILES WEVER TODD PRIZE

The editors at Pleiades Press select 10-15 finalists from among those manuscripts submitted each year. A judge of national renown selects one winner for publication. All selections are made blind to authorship in a contest in an open competition for which any poet writing in English is eligible. Lena-Miles Wever Todd prize-winning books are distributed by Louisiana State University Press.

ALSO AVAILABLE FROM PLEIADES PRESS

Book of No Ledge by Nance Van Winckel

Landscape with Headless Mama by Jennifer Givhan

Random Exorcisms by Adrian C. Louis

Poetry Comics from the Book of Hours by Bianca Stone

The Belle Mar by Katie Bickham

Sylph by Abigail Cloud

The Glacier's Wake by Katy Didden

Paradise, Indiana by Bruce Snider

What's this, Bombardier? by Ryan Flaherty

Self-Portrait with Expletives by Kevin Clark

Pacific Shooter by Susan Parr

It was a terrible cloud at twilight by Alessandra Lynch

Compulsions of Silkworms & Bees by Julianna Baggott

Snow House by Brian Swann

Motherhouse by Kathleen Jesme

Lure by Nils Michals

The Green Girls by John Blair

A Sacrificial Zinc by Matthew Cooperman

The Light in Our House by Al Maginnes

Strange Wood by Kevin Prufer

PLEIADES
P R E S S